CODING ADVENTURES WITH PYTHON AND PYCHARM FOR KIDS

Unlocking the Magic of Coding: A Kid's Guide
to Python Adventures with PyCharm

Ghada Atef

To all the young minds out there who are curious, creative, and courageous.

To the dreamers who look up at the stars and wonder how they shine, to the adventurers who aren't afraid to ask 'why' and 'how', and to the magicians who believe in the power of words and numbers to create new worlds - this book is for you.

May your journey into the world of coding be filled with exciting challenges, triumphant victories, and the joy of continuous learning. Remember, every great coder started out with a single line of code, just like you.

Happy Coding!

"The computer was born to solve problems that did not exist before."

BILL GATES

CONTENTS

PREFACE

Welcome to "Coding Adventures with Python and PyCharm for Kids: Unlocking the Magic of Coding: A Kid's Guide to Python Adventures with PyCharm". This book is not just about learning to code, it's about embarking on an adventure into the world of creativity, problem-solving, and endless possibilities.

Coding is a superpower. With it, you can build worlds, solve puzzles, and bring your ideas to life. Python, a powerful yet simple programming language, and PyCharm, a versatile integrated development environment, are your tools on this journey.

This book is designed to be your guide, your map, and your companion on this adventure. It will introduce you to the basics of Python and PyCharm, guide you through the process of building your first programs, and challenge you with exciting projects.

Remember, every coder was once a beginner. Don't be afraid to make mistakes, ask questions, and try new things. That's how we learn, grow, and become better coders.

So, are you ready to unlock the magic of coding? Let's start this adventure!

Happy Coding!

PROLOGUE

Once upon a time, in a world not so different from ours, there was a language that could bring ideas to life. This language, known as Python, was not spoken by people, but by computers. And those who could speak it were known as coders.

In this book, "Coding Adventures with Python and PyCharm for Kids: Unlocking the Magic of Coding: A Kid's Guide to Python Adventures with PyCharm", you will learn this magical language. But more than that, you will embark on an adventure. An adventure that will take you from being a novice to a confident coder.

Along the way, you will encounter challenges, puzzles, and tasks that will test your skills and creativity. But fear not, for you will not be alone. PyCharm, a powerful tool used by coders around the world, will be your companion.

So, prepare yourself for an adventure like no other. An adventure where you will unlock the magic of coding and discover a world of endless possibilities.

Let the adventure begin!

CONTACT ME

Thank you for grabbing a copy of my book **Coding Adventures with Python and PyCharm for Kids!** I hope you found the book informative and helpful on your journey.

If you have any questions, comments, or suggestions, please feel free to contact me through the following channels:

Email: [linux.expert.eg@gmail.com]

Social Media:

[https://www.linkedin.com/in/ghada-atef/]

I strive to respond to all inquiries within 48 hours.

I am always looking for ways to improve my work, so your feedback is greatly appreciated. Thank you for helping me make this book the best it can be!

INTRODUCTION

Welcome to the World of Coding!

Welcome, young adventurers, to the enchanting world of programming!

Imagine being able to create your own worlds, filled with characters and creatures that move and interact according to your commands. Imagine being able to solve complex puzzles, design beautiful patterns, or even build your own.

CHAPTER 1: WHAT IS PROGRAMMING? WHY LEARN PYTHON? WHAT IS PYCHARM?

Section 1: The Enchanting World of Programming

Welcome to the Enthralling Universe of Coding!

Embark on a journey into the captivating world of coding, where words transform into the building blocks of enchanting castles, and computers become your powerful allies. Coding is the art of crafting clear and precise instructions, akin to creating a well-written recipe, to command your computer ally through incredible tasks step by step.

Picture a scenario where your computer is a super-powered companion, capable of flawlessly executing your instructions. Coding empowers you to communicate with this ally in a secret language, allowing you to bring your innovative ideas to life on the screen.

With coding, you open the door to a realm of possibilities:

1. Create games and animations: Bring characters to life by making them move, jump, and dance. Imagine a game where your character must navigate obstacles to earn points.

Example: You can design a game where a spaceship dodges asteroids, collecting energy crystals along the way.

2. Build websites and apps: Design interactive experiences for others to enjoy. Develop a website for your school's science club or an app that helps people **Remember** important dates.

Example: Create an app that sends reminders for homework deadlines, ensuring students stay organized.

3. Solve mysteries and puzzles: Utilize coding skills to decipher codes and uncover hidden secrets. Develop a program that can solve Sudoku puzzles in seconds.

Example: Write a program that decrypts messages for a spy-themed puzzle game.

4. Become a digital artist: Use code as your brush to create stunning pictures and patterns. Develop a digital art piece that changes dynamically with user interaction.

Example: Craft an interactive digital painting where colors shift based on the user's input.

The most exhilarating part? Coding is like acquiring a new superpower, allowing you to transform ideas into reality and breathe life into anything you can envision on the screen.

Are you ready to unlock the magic of coding and embark on thrilling adventures? Let's plunge into the fascinating world of Python and PyCharm!

Section 2: Python and PyCharm - Your Coding Companions

Why Python and PyCharm Are Your Ultimate Coding Companions!

Prepare for an exhilarating journey into the world of coding with two remarkable companions: Python and PyCharm.

Python: Your Friendly Coding Language Guide

Imagine learning a language that communicates not in words but in simple instructions understood by computers. Python, your friendly coding language guide, is renowned for its beginner-friendly nature, like a patient and supportive mentor.

- Easy to read and write: Python uses familiar words and phrases, making it feel more like giving clear commands than memorizing complex code. For instance, printing "Hello, World!" is as simple as writing `print("Hello, World!")`.

Example: Write a program that prompts the user for their name and greets them with a personalized message.

- Powerful and versatile: Despite its beginner-friendly demeanor, Python can create a wide array of cool things, from games and animations to websites and scientific programs. Even NASA relies on Python for their programming needs.

Example: Develop a program that simulates the motion of planets in a solar system.

- Huge community: Join millions of Python enthusiasts worldwide, ensuring that help and support are always available online. Numerous forums and websites are dedicated to assisting Python learners.

Example: Solve coding challenges on platforms like LeetCode and share your solutions with the Python community.

PyCharm: Your Magical Coding Toolkit

Consider PyCharm your personal coding assistant, helping you write code more efficiently and avoid mistakes.

- Highlights your code: PyCharm acts like a highlighter, automatically indicating if you've missed something or made a typo, making it easier to catch errors before running your program.

Example: Intentionally introduce an error in your code and let PyCharm guide you to find and fix it.

- Suggests what to write next: Similar to a good friend finishing your sentences, PyCharm suggests code based on what you've already typed, known as "code completion."

Example: Begin coding a simple calculator, and let PyCharm assist you in completing the mathematical operations.

- Keeps you organized: As your projects grow, PyCharm helps you keep your code neat and comprehensible, acting as a super-powered filing cabinet for all your coding ideas. Efficiently manage your files and folders.

Example: Create a project to build a basic website, and let PyCharm organize your files for easy navigation.

Together, **Python** and **PyCharm** form a dream team for your coding adventures. They make learning enjoyable, assist in creating amazing things, and guide you on your journey to becoming a coding maestro. Ready to embark on your coding quest with these fantastic companions by your side? Let's get started!

CHAPTER 2: PYTHON PLAYGROUND

Section 1: Gently introduce Python through interactive exercises and puzzles.

Let's Play with Words and Make the Computer Dance!

Welcome to your first steps in the amazing world of coding with Python! Today, we'll have some fun using words and simple commands to make the computer do our bidding. Think of it like training a special pet that understands our instructions, just like a dog understands "sit" or "fetch"!

Puzzle 1: Word Detective

The computer loves to understand patterns, just like a detective loves to solve mysteries! Can you help it figure out these riddles? Write down your answers and see if the computer agrees:

1. I have 3 letters, and I mean the opposite of hot. What am I?
Answer: Cold

2. I have 4 letters, and I'm the first thing you do in the morning (not counting sleeping!). What am I?
Answer: Wake

3. I have 5 letters, and I'm something you wear on your feet. What am I?
Answer: Shoes

Bonus: Can you think of your own riddles for the computer? Write them down and try them out! For example, "I have 4 letters, and I'm something you use to write. What am I?"

Your Riddle: [Write your own riddle here]

Puzzle 2: Drawing Shapes with Words

Did you know you can use words to tell the computer to draw pictures? Let's try! Imagine you have a turtle friend who can move forward, turn left or right, and even pick up its pen to draw. Here are some commands to try:

- `forward 100`: This tells the turtle to move forward 100 steps, just like you would walk forward.

- `left 90`: This turns the turtle 90 degrees to the left, like turning a corner on a square block.

- `right 90`: This turns the turtle 90 degrees to the right, like turning a corner on a square block in the opposite direction.

- `pen down`: This tells the turtle to put its pen down and start drawing, like when you start writing with a pen on paper.

- `pen up`: This tells the turtle to lift its pen and stop drawing, like when you finish writing a sentence.

Can you use these commands to draw a square, a triangle, or even a star? **Remember**, you can experiment and try different things! For example, to draw a square, you could use the commands `forward 100`, `right 90`, `forward 100`, `right 90`, `forward 100`, `right 90`, `forward 100`.

Remember:

- Don't worry if you get stuck. Experiment, try new things, and have fun! Coding is like solving puzzles and figuring out how things work.

- The more you practice, the better you'll become at giving the computer clear instructions, just like how practicing a musical instrument makes you better at playing it.

- These are just the first steps in your coding adventure with Python. Keep practicing, keep exploring, and soon you'll be creating amazing things with your newfound coding skills.

Section 2: Cover basic syntax, variables, data types, and simple operations.

Building Your Coding Toolbox: Words, Names, and Magic Tricks!

Get ready to embark on exciting coding adventures with Python and PyCharm! In this section, we'll unlock the magic of coding by exploring some essential tools in our coding toolbox. Think of them as special ingredients that help us cook up awesome programs!

Words with Power:

Imagine you're giving instructions to a robot chef. You wouldn't just say "make food," right? You'd tell it exactly what to do: "Chop the vegetables," "Add water to the pot," or "Stir for five minutes." In coding, we use similar instructions, like "print('Hello, world!')" to display a message or "move_forward(100)" to make a character move on the screen.

Numbers and Names:

Numbers aren't just for counting! They help us store information, like a character's health points in a game (e.g., 100) or the size of a circle we want to draw (e.g., 50). Just like we give nicknames to our friends, we can also give names to these numbers. For example, instead of writing "100" everywhere, we can call it "health" or "circle_size" for easier understanding. These named numbers are called variables.

Variable Magic:

Imagine a treasure chest where you can store anything you want. In coding, variables are like these chests. You give them a name (like "treasure") and store things inside, like numbers (gold coins!), words (secret messages), or even pictures (a magical map)! This way, you can easily refer to them later without having to write everything out again.

Data Types: Sorting Our Stuff

Just like you wouldn't put books in your shoebox, in coding, we have different types of boxes (called data types) for different kinds of things:

- Numbers: These boxes hold numbers, like how many lives you have left in a game (integers) or the precise location of a character on the screen (decimals).

- Text: These boxes hold words and sentences, like the dialogue in your game (strings) or the username you choose when you start playing.

- True or False: These boxes can only hold either "True" or "False," like checking if a key is pressed on the keyboard or if a guess in your quiz is correct.

Simple Operations: Putting It All Together

Now that we have our tools, let's learn some basic tricks! We can use special symbols called operators to do things like:

- Plus (+): Combine things, like adding points to your score or joining two shapes together. Imagine collecting coins in a game: score += 10 adds 10 points to your current score.

- Minus (-): Take things away, like losing health in a game or erasing part of a drawing. Imagine getting hit by an enemy: health -= 5 removes 5 health points.

- Equals (=): Assign values to variables, like storing your name in a game or the current level you're on. Imagine starting a new level:

level = 2 sets the level number to 2.

Remember:

- Coding is like learning a new language. The more you practice, the better you'll become at understanding and using these building blocks to create amazing things!

- Don't be afraid to experiment and make mistakes. That's how we learn and grow as coders.

- We'll gradually introduce more complex concepts as you progress on your coding adventure. Just keep exploring, have fun, and enjoy the process of learning and creating!

Section 3: Utilize colorful visuals and age-appropriate examples to engage children.

Welcome, young inventor, to your very own coding workshop! Imagine you have a box of magical building blocks, each one a special word or symbol that unlocks incredible powers. With these blocks, you can tell the computer exactly what you want it to do, and just like a friendly robot friend, it will follow your instructions to create amazing things!

Let's Explore Our Toolbox:

Instruction Blocks: These colorful commands are the lifeblood of your code, like puzzle pieces that snap together to bring your ideas to life. Imagine a blue block saying "move forward" to make your game character walk, or a green block saying "draw a circle" to create a bouncing ball. Explore different colored blocks to discover even more

Exciting commands!

Number Blocks: These hold valuable numbers, like the points you collect in your game or the size of a shape you want to draw. Think of them as treasure chests filled with numerical goodies! You can use them to count lives, measure distances, or even store secret codes.

Name Tags: Just like we give nicknames to our friends, we can use special name tags called variables to identify things we store in our code, like "score" or "player_name." Imagine them as sticky notes you can use to label your coding treasures, making them easier to find and reuse later.

Variable Magic: Remember those treasure chests with name tags? Well, variables are like magical vaults where you can store anything you want: numbers, words, even pictures! This way, you can easily refer to them later without having to repeat everything. Think of it as having a special box for your "high score" that you can update as you play, making your game more interactive!

Data Type Detectives: We wouldn't put cookies in a jewelry box, would we? In coding, we have different types of boxes (called data types) for different kinds of treasures:

Number Boxes: These sturdy safes hold your numerical riches, like your game score or the size of a shape. Imagine them keeping track of your collected coins or the distance your rocket ship has traveled!

Text Boxes: These colorful storybooks hold exciting words and sentences, like your character's name in a story or a message you want to display on the screen. Imagine using them to create funny dialogue for your characters or display helpful instructions for your game!

True/False Boxes: These special coin boxes can only hold either "True" or "False," like checking if a button is pressed or if a guess in your quiz is correct. Use them to create interactive elements in your game, like doors that only open if you solve a puzzle!

Operation Time! Putting It All Together:

Now that you have your tools, let's learn some cool tricks! We can use special symbols called operators to do amazing things:

- **Plus (+):** This magic wand makes your treasures grow bigger! Use it to combine shapes, add points to your score, or increase your character's speed.

- **Minus (-):** This shrinking potion makes your treasures smaller! Use it to erase part of a drawing, lose health in a game, or decrease the difficulty of a level.

- **Equals (=):** This special marker labels your treasures with their magical properties! Use it to store your username, the current level you're on, or any other important information.

Remember:

- Coding is like a grand adventure where you're the captain, sailing across a sea of possibilities with your colorful blocks and magical tools. Don't be afraid to experiment, mix and match, and see what incredible creations you can build. As you explore further, we'll gradually introduce more complex tools and challenges to keep your coding journey exciting!

- The most important thing is to have fun, explore, and enjoy the magic of creating with code!

Section 4: Gradually introduce conditional statements and loops with real-world scenarios.

Unleash Even More Power!

You've mastered some amazing coding skills already! But what if your creations could make choices, react to situations, and even perform actions repeatedly? That's where conditional statements and loops come in, like sprinkling magical ingredients into your coding recipe!

Making Decisions Like a Superhero (with Conditional Statements):

Imagine you're designing a superhero game. When your hero encounters a villain, you want them to react differently based on their powers. That's where if statements swoop in! They act like decision points in your code, asking questions like:

"If the hero has super strength, can they break through the wall?"

"If the villain is invisible, can the hero use their special detector?"

Think of them as magic switches that turn different parts of your code on or off depending on the answer, making your game more interactive and exciting!

Example:

```
if hero_power == "super_strength":
    print("The hero smashes through the wall!")
elif hero_power == "laser_vision":
    print("The hero blasts the villain with lasers!")
```

else:

    print("The hero needs to think of another plan!")

Repeating Actions Like a Robot on a Mission (with Loops):

Now, imagine you want your robot character to collect coins scattered across a room until it finds them all. That's where loops come in! They're like supercharged commands that let you repeat a block of code over and over until a certain condition is met, just like a robot following instructions.

Example:

while coins_collected < total_coins:

    move_forward()

check_for_coins()

print("The robot found all the coins! Hooray!")

Cool Uses in the Real World:

These coding tools are like secret codes that power many things around you! For example:

Traffic lights: They use conditional statements to change color based on time or the presence of cars, keeping us safe on the road.

Washing machines: They use loops to spin clothes for a set time or until they're clean, ensuring your clothes are fresh and ready to wear.

Video games: Both are used to create different levels, enemy behavior, and player responses, making the games fun and engaging.

Remember:

- **Start small:** Begin with simple examples like choosing between two options or repeating a movement a few times.

- **Experiment bravely:** Don't be afraid to try different things and see what happens! Coding is all about exploration and learning from mistakes.

- **Have fun!** The most important thing is to enjoy the process of creating and seeing your code come to life.

CHAPTER 3: GETTING STARTED WITH PYCHARM

Section 1: Enter PyCharm,
Your Coding Ally

Welcome, young coding adventurer! Get ready to embark on an exciting journey with Python and your new best friend, PyCharm! Think of PyCharm as your personal coding playground, filled with tools and tricks to bring your creative ideas to life. But it's not just a playground – it's also your superhero ally, helping you write code efficiently, solve problems like a champion, and unlock the full potential of Python!

Here's how PyCharm will be your trusty companion on your coding adventures:

Your Customized Coding HQ:

Imagine a cool, personalized workspace where everything is just the way you like it, with all your coding tools easily accessible. That's what PyCharm gives you! You can arrange different windows, choose themes that make your eyes happy, and keep everything organized, just like your favorite superhero setting up their secret headquarters.

Supercharged Code-Writing Tools:

Just like any superhero has cool gadgets, PyCharm comes with its own set of awesome tools to make coding faster, easier, and more fun! Imagine features like:

Code completion: This is like having a helpful friend who suggests what to write next, saving you time and typing.

Error highlighting: Think of it as a friendly warning system that points out mistakes before they become problems, helping you write cleaner code.

Smart formatting: Imagine your code magically tidying itself up, making it easier to read and understand, just like a superhero keeping their gear organized.

Your Friendly Coding Coach:

Ever get stuck on a tricky coding puzzle? Not to worry! PyCharm is like your personal coding coach, always there to offer helpful hints and suggestions. It can explain things in a clear way, answer your questions, and guide you back on the right track, just like a wise mentor helping you overcome obstacles.

Unlocking Python's Secrets:

Think of Python as a powerful language with hidden secrets. PyCharm understands Python inside and out, so it can help you use it to its full potential. It can suggest the right words and phrases, remind you of useful commands, and even explain how things work behind the scenes, just like a skilled decoder unlocking the secrets of a mysterious message.

Join the Coding Community:

The world of coding is vast and exciting, but you don't have to explore it alone! PyCharm connects you to a community of other young coders, just like finding a team of awesome friends in a superhero movie. You can share your creations, ask questions, get help, and even inspire each other, making your coding journey even more fun and rewarding.

Ready to Start Your Coding Adventure?

With PyCharm as your partner, no coding challenge is too big! So, grab your coding cape, fire up PyCharm, and get ready to create amazing things! **Remember**, the most important thing is to have fun, explore, and enjoy the magic of coding. Let's unlock your coding potential together!

Section 2: Showcase PyCharm's colorful interface and user-friendly features.

Dive right into PyCharm's exciting playground, where your coding dreams transform into reality! Think of it as your personal coding haven, filled with vibrant colors, helpful tools, and endless possibilities. Get ready to explore its unique features:

A Rainbow of Code Clarity: Imagine your code looking like a vibrant masterpiece! PyCharm paints different parts of your code in distinct colors, making it like a beautifully organized rainbow. This helps you understand what each line does at a glance, making coding easier and more enjoyable.

Smart Helpers at Your Fingertips: Feeling lost in the middle of writing code? No worries! PyCharm has your back with its friendly helper pop-ups. These little reminders suggest what you might type next, acting like whispering code coaches guiding you along the way. Never get stuck again with these helpful hints!

Code Completion Magic: Your Time-Saving Genie! Ever start typing and forget the next step? PyCharm comes to the rescue! Its superpowered autocomplete **Remember**s your code patterns and suggests what you might be writing, saving you time and frustration. It's like having a personal genie that predicts your coding wishes!

Customize Your Coding Wonderland: Make PyCharm your own! Change the colors, fonts, and even the layout to match your style and personality. Think of it like decorating your own coding room

– make it as comfortable and inspiring as possible for your coding adventures!

Explore with Ease: Curiosity is Always Welcome! Wondering what a specific symbol or command does? Simply hover your mouse over it, and PyCharm will magically display a helpful explanation. It's like having a built-in encyclopedia of coding knowledge readily available at your fingertips!

Remember, PyCharm is designed to make your coding journey fun, easy, and empowering. So don't be afraid to experiment, explore, and unleash your creativity! With PyCharm as your partner, the only limit is your imagination. Let's start coding and witness the incredible things you can create!

Section 3: Explain projects, files, and the editor in a simplified manner.

Ready to embark on your epic coding adventure? Just like any hero needs their tools and map, you'll use three key things in your coding journey: projects, files, and the editor. Don't worry, they're simpler than they sound!

Imagine Projects as Your Grand Adventures:

Think of a project as the big story you're creating with code. It could be anything your imagination cooks up, like building a pizza-ordering game, animating a dancing robot, or even designing a website for your pet cat! Each project holds all the parts you need to make your idea come to life, just like a treasure map leading you to hidden riches.

Files: Your Handy Toolbox:

Imagine files as the special tools you use in your project. Each file holds a specific piece of your code, like instructions for moving your game character, drawing colorful shapes, or storing information like player scores. It's like having a hammer for building a house, a paintbrush for creating art, and a

wrench for fixing things, all neatly organized in your toolbox.

The Editor: Your Coding Playground:

This is where the magic happens! The editor is where you write and arrange your code files, just like putting together the pieces of your project. It has cool features like color-coding different parts of your code to make it easier to read, and even suggests what you might want to type next like a helpful friend! Think of it as a fun and organized workbench where you bring your coding creations to life.

Remember, Every Hero Starts Small:

Don't get discouraged if things seem tricky at first! Just like learning any new skill, coding takes practice and exploration. But with a little bit of perseverance and a lot of creativity, you'll be using projects, files, and the editor like a pro in no time! So, grab your coding tools, unlock your imagination, and get ready to create amazing things!

CHAPTER 4: SETTING UP YOUR CODING SPACE IN PYCHARM

Section 1: Guide children through creating their first PyCharm project step-by-step

Welcome, young coding explorer! Are you ready to unlock the magic of Python and unleash your creativity? Today, you'll take your first steps in PyCharm, your powerful coding companion, to create your very own Python program! Let's dive in:

Step 1: Download and Install Your Coding Ally
Imagine PyCharm as your personal spaceship that blasts you into the exciting world of coding! To download it, visit the official JetBrains website [https://www.jetbrains.com/pycharm/] with a grown-up's help. Click the "Download" button and choose the free "Community Edition". Once downloaded, follow the instructions to install it on your computer.

Step 2: Launch Your Coding Starship!
Open PyCharm, and you'll see a friendly welcome screen. Click the "Create New Project" button, like setting off on a new coding adventure!

Step 3: Name Your Coding Mission
A window appears where you can name your project. Think of it as naming your spaceship! Let's call it "MyAwesomeProject" (or choose a name that reflects your coding dream). Make sure the "Base interpreter" is set to Python, your fuel for coding magic.

Step 4: Craft Your First Coding Tool
Now, you're inside PyCharm! Right-click on your project name on

the left (think of it as your spaceship's control panel) and select "New" followed by "Python File". Name this file "main.py", like your main coding tool for this mission.

Step 5: Write Your First Code Spell!
Inside "main.py", you'll write your first Python code, like casting a magical spell! Type the following lines:

```
print("Hello, World!")
```

This code tells your computer to display the message "Hello, World!" on the screen. It's your first step towards becoming a coding wizard!

Step 6: Blast Off Your Code!
To run your code, right-click anywhere in "main.py" and choose "Run 'main'". Imagine pressing the launch button on your spaceship! If everything is correct, you'll see "Hello, World!" appear in the output window at the bottom, like receiving a message from your code!

Congratulations, young coding adventurer! You've created and run your first Python program in PyCharm. This marks the beginning of your coding journey filled with endless possibilities. Keep exploring, experiment, and have fun! **Remember**, the only limit is your imagination!

Section 2: Start with simple tasks like printing text and drawing shapes.

Ready to start bringing your coding ideas to life? Let's begin with some fun and fundamental tasks in Python!

1. Speak Up, Python! Printing Messages:

Imagine you're building a robot friend. How would you make it speak? In Python, we use the print command to display messages like this:

```
print("Hello, world! I'm your robot friend!")
```

Run this code, and you'll see the greeting appear on your screen, just like your robot saying hello! Cool, right?

2. Draw Like a Master Artist: Creating Shapes:

Python lets you become a digital artist! We can use the turtle module to draw all sorts of shapes. Here's how to draw a square:

```
import turtle

# Create a colorful canvas
screen = turtle.Screen()
screen.bgcolor("light green")

# Meet our artist, "square"
square = turtle.Turtle()
```

```
# Let's draw!
for _ in range(4):
    square.forward(100) # Move forward 100 steps
    square.right(90)  # Turn right 90 degrees

# Keep the masterpiece open
screen.exitonclick()
```

Run this code, and you'll see a beautiful square appear! Feeling creative? Change the number in range(4) to draw different shapes:

- range(3) for a triangle

- range(5) for a pentagon

Explore further numbers to discover more shapes!

Remember, practice is the key to coding magic. Keep experimenting, try different colors, and draw amazing things!

Section 3: Gradually introduce more complex concepts such as functions, modules, and debugging.

So, you've mastered printing text and drawing shapes? Time to step up your coding game with superpowers like functions, modules, and debugging!

1. Functions: Your Code Super Soldiers!

Imagine you have a group of helpful robot friends. You can tell them to do specific tasks, right? In Python, functions are like your code robots! You create them once, and they can be called again and again to perform the same task.

Here's a function that greets someone:

```
def greet(name):
    print(f"Hello, {name}!")
```

Think of greet as your robot's name. We give it a "name" (Python calls it a parameter) and when you call greet("Alice"), your robot springs into action, saying "Hello, Alice!". Neat, huh?

2. Modules: Code Libraries for Sharing Powers!

Remember your robot friends? Sometimes, they need extra tools for specific jobs. In Python, modules are like toolboxes full of pre-made code (functions and variables) for different tasks. You can "borrow" them to save time and effort.

For example, the math module has tools for doing calculations.

We can "import" it and use its "pi" value:

import math

print(math.pi) # Prints 3.14159...

Now you can use pi in your code, just like using a built-in tool!

3. Debugging: Catching Code Gremlins!

Even the best superheroes make mistakes sometimes. In coding, those mistakes are called bugs. But don't worry, you have a superpower too: debugging!

Think of debugging as having a special tool to examine your code and find these bugs. PyCharm, your coding partner, has a built-in debugger. Think of it like a code scanner! You can set a "breakpoint" (like a marker) and run your code step-by-step, seeing what's happening inside. This helps you find the bug and fix it!

Remember, learning to code is a journey, just like any adventure. There will be challenges, but with practice, patience, and your new superpowers, you can overcome them and create amazing things!

CHAPTER 5: EXPLORING PYTHON BASICS IN PYCHARM

Section 1: Dive into Python fundamentals: Variables and Data Types, Operators, Control Flow (If Statements, For and While Loops), Functions

Variables and Data Types

In Python, a variable is like a box for storing data values. Unlike other programming languages, Python doesn't require a special command for declaring a variable. A variable is created the moment you first assign a value to it. For example:

x = 5 # Here, x is a variable of type 'int' (integer)

y = "Hello, World!" # Here, y is a variable of type 'str' (string)

Python has several built-in data types, categorized as follows:

- **Text Type:** `str` (for text strings)

- **Numeric Types:** `int` (for whole numbers), `float` (for decimal numbers), `complex` (for complex numbers)

- **Sequence Types:** `list` (an ordered collection), `tuple` (an ordered, immutable collection), `range` (a sequence of numbers)

- **Mapping Type:** `dict` (a collection of key-value pairs)

- **Set Types:** `set` (an unordered collection of unique elements), `frozenset` (an immutable set)

- **Boolean Type:** `bool` (represents True or False)

- **Binary Types:** `bytes`, `bytearray`, `memoryview` (used for manipulating binary data)

Operators

Operators are special symbols used to perform operations on variables and values. Python categorizes operators into the following groups:

- **Arithmetic operators:** such as + (addition), - (subtraction), * (multiplication), / (division), and % (modulus)

- **Assignment operators:** such as = (assigns value), += (adds and assigns), and -= (subtracts and assigns)

- **Comparison operators:** such as == (equal), != (not equal), < (less than), and > (greater than)

- **Logical operators:** `and`, `or`, `not`

- **Identity operators:** `is`, `is not`

- **Membership operators:** `in`, `not in`

- **Bitwise operators:** & (and), | (or), ^ (xor), ~ (not), << (left shift), >> (right shift)

Control Flow

1. If Statements

An "if statement" is written by using the `if` keyword. For example:

a = 33

b = 200

if b > a:

  print("b is greater than a")

For and While Loops

A `for` loop is used for iterating over a sequence (that is either a list, a tuple, a dictionary, a set, or a string). For example:

fruits = ["apple", "banana", "cherry"]
for x in fruits:
  print(x)

2. A `while` loop executes a set of statements as long as a condition is true. For example:

i = 1
while i < 6:
  print(i)
  i += 1

Functions

A function is a block of code which only runs when it is called. You can pass data, known as parameters, into a function. A function can return data as a result. For example:

def my_function():
  print("Hello from a function")

my_function() # This calls the function, causing it to run

Real-life Example: Imagine creating a function `calculate_score` that takes player performance data as parameters and returns the calculated score.

With these fundamentals, you're well-equipped to begin your coding journey in Python!

Section 2: Emphasize the connection between Python basics and coding in PyCharm.

Connecting Python Basics with PyCharm

PyCharm, an Integrated Development Environment (IDE), serves as a powerful tool for programming in Python. Beyond a mere text editor, PyCharm offers an array of features such as code analysis, a graphical debugger, integrated unit testing, and robust support for web development with Django. Let's explore how the fundamentals of Python seamlessly integrate with the coding experience in PyCharm.

Variables and Data Types

In PyCharm, creating variables is not just about assigning values; the IDE intelligently recognizes the data type, enhancing your coding efficiency. Moreover, features like auto-completion and in-line debugging provide invaluable assistance during coding.

Real-life Example: Imagine you are developing a game in PyCharm, and as you create a variable `player_score`, PyCharm recognizes it as an integer, offering helpful suggestions and hints as you continue coding.

Operators

PyCharm goes beyond being a mere code editor; it assists you in managing operator precedence. It highlights potential issues and offers quick-fix suggestions to ensure your code runs smoothly.

Real-life Example: Suppose you are implementing a complex mathematical algorithm in PyCharm, and it identifies a potential issue with operator precedence, guiding you to the correct solution.

Control Flow

PyCharm enhances the readability of your code by providing visual cues and indentation guides for control flow statements like if statements and loops. This feature ensures that your code is well-structured and easy to understand.

Real-life Example: As you write an if statement in PyCharm to check whether a certain condition is met, the IDE visually guides you with indentation, making your code visually appealing and logically organized.

Functions

When defining functions in PyCharm, the IDE not only checks the syntax but also allows you to navigate to the function definition effortlessly and view quick documentation.

Real-life Example: As you create a function to handle user authentication in a PyCharm project, the IDE offers quick documentation, helping you understand the purpose and parameters of the function instantly.

Debugging in PyCharm

PyCharm offers a powerful debugging feature that allows you to set breakpoints and step through your Python code line by line. This functionality aids in understanding the code execution process and tracking variable values, providing a robust method for debugging.

Real-life Example: You are developing a web application in PyCharm, and by setting breakpoints, you can analyze the flow of your code and identify any issues in real-time.

Remember, as you embark on your coding adventure, PyCharm serves as more than just a text editor—it's a complete development environment with powerful tools for Python programming.

CHAPTER 6: DIVING DEEPER INTO PYTHON WITH PYCHARM

Section 1: Explore Lists, Tuples, and Dictionaries

Exploring Lists, Tuples, and Dictionaries

Lists

A list in Python is a versatile collection of items that maintains order and allows for modifications. Lists can contain duplicate members, making them useful for various scenarios.

 # Creating a list

fruits = ["apple", "banana", "cherry"]

print(fruits)

This will output: `['apple', 'banana', 'cherry']`

Real-life Example: Imagine you are building a shopping cart application. The list `cart_items` can store the names of items, and it can be easily modified to add or remove products.

Tuples

A tuple in Python is a structured collection of items that maintains order and, unlike lists, is immutable (unchangeable). Tuples can also contain duplicate members.

 # Creating a tuple

fruits = ("apple", "banana", "cherry")

print(fruits)

This will output: `('apple', 'banana', 'cherry')`

Real-life Example: Consider a scenario where you need to store the coordinates of a fixed set of locations. The tuple `location_coordinates` can efficiently represent this data without the risk of unintentional modifications.

Dictionaries

A dictionary in Python is a dynamic collection of items that is unordered, changeable, and indexed. Unlike lists and tuples, dictionaries use key-value pairs and do not allow duplicate keys.

```
# Creating a dictionary
car = {
  "brand": "Ford",
  "model": "Mustang",
  "year": 1964
}
print(car)
```

This will output: `{'brand': 'Ford', 'model': 'Mustang', 'year': 1964}`

Real-life Example: Suppose you are developing a contact book application. The dictionary `contact_info` can store details about each person using keys like "name," "phone," and "email," providing an efficient way to access and modify specific information.

In PyCharm, a powerful Integrated Development Environment (IDE), you can easily create and manipulate these data structures with features such as code completion and quick documentation.

Real-life Example: While coding in PyCharm, imagine you are designing a program that uses a dictionary to manage user preferences. PyCharm's code completion and quick documentation features can help you efficiently explore and utilize the available keys and values within the dictionary.

As you embark on your coding adventure, understanding and mastering these fundamental data structures will empower you to build diverse and dynamic Python applications with ease.

Section 2: Cover File I/O and Error Handling.

File I/O and Error Handling

File I/O

File Input/Output (I/O) is a critical aspect of programming in Python, enabling the creation, reading, updating, and deletion of files.

Creating a File

To create a file, utilize the `open()` function with the 'w' mode. If the file already exists, the 'w' mode will overwrite its contents.

file = open('myfile.txt', 'w')

file.write('Hello, world!')

file.close()

Real-life Example: Imagine you are developing a program to save user preferences. The 'w' mode can be employed to create a configuration file where user settings are stored.

Reading a File

To read a file, open it in 'r' mode and use the `read()` function to access its contents.

file = open('myfile.txt', 'r')

print(file.read())

file.close()

Real-life Example: Consider an application where you store game levels in a file. The 'r' mode can be utilized to read the file and load the levels into the game dynamically.

Error Handling

Errors are an inevitable part of programming. Python provides mechanisms to handle errors and exceptions that may occur during program execution.

Try/Except

A try/except block allows you to catch exceptions and handle them gracefully.

try:

  print(x)

except:

  print("An error occurred")

In this example, Python attempts to print the variable x. If x does not exist, an error would typically halt the program. However, the try/except block catches the error, allowing the program to continue running and printing "An error occurred" instead.

Real-life Example: Imagine a scenario where your program fetches data from an online source. Using try/except, you can gracefully handle network errors, ensuring that the program doesn't crash if there's a connection issue.

Remember, PyCharm enhances your coding experience with features like syntax highlighting and error detection, aiding in more efficient Python program development and debugging.

Real-life Example: While coding in PyCharm, consider writing a program that manipulates files. The IDE's features, such as syntax highlighting, help you spot potential errors, while error detection ensures you address issues promptly, creating robust and error-free code.

CHAPTER 7:
UNLEASHING
PYCHARM FEATURES

Section 1: Uncover PyCharm features: Code Completion, Debugging Tools, Refactoring Code, Using Version Control

Uncovering PyCharm Features

Code Completion

Code completion, also known as autocompletion, is a feature that predicts and provides a list of possible variables, methods, classes, etc. as you type. This feature saves time by preventing the need to type out entire words and helps eliminate typos.

 # When you start typing 'pri', PyCharm will suggest 'print'.

pri

Real-life Example: Imagine you are working on a project and need to use a specific library function, such as 'matplotlib.pyplot.' With code completion in PyCharm, you can quickly access and insert the function without memorizing the entire name.

Debugging Tools

Debugging is the process of finding and resolving defects or problems within a program. PyCharm offers various debugging tools to streamline this process. You can set breakpoints, step through your code, inspect variables, and more.

 # Set a breakpoint at this line and start debugging.

```
print("Hello, World!")
```

Real-life Example: Picture yourself developing a game where the scoring mechanism isn't working as expected. With PyCharm's debugging tools, you can set breakpoints, analyze variable values, and identify the source of the issue efficiently.

Refactoring Code

Refactoring is the process of restructuring existing code without altering its external behavior. PyCharm provides tools for refactoring, such as renaming symbols and extracting methods or variables.

```
# Right-click on 'my_function' and select 'Refactor' -> 'Rename' to rename the function.
def my_function():
    print("Hello from a function")
```

Real-life Example: Consider a scenario where you need to change the name of a function across your entire project. Using PyCharm's refactoring tools, you can rename the function seamlessly, ensuring consistency in your codebase.

Using Version Control

Version control systems help manage changes to source code over time. PyCharm has built-in support for version control systems like Git, allowing you to commit changes, create branches, merge code, and more.

```
# PyCharm provides a 'Version Control' tab where you can see all your changes.
print("Hello, World!")
```

Real-life Example: In a collaborative project, you and your team are working on different features simultaneously. With PyCharm's version control integration, you can easily track changes, commit updates, and collaborate seamlessly with others.

Remember, PyCharm is more than just a text editor—it's a comprehensive development environment offering powerful tools for Python programming.

CHAPTER 8: PRO TIPS AND TRICKS FOR YOUNG CODERS

Section 1: Share helpful shortcuts and keyboard combinations

Helpful Shortcuts and Keyboard Combinations

PyCharm provides a plethora of keyboard shortcuts to enhance your coding efficiency. Here are some of the most useful ones:

General Shortcuts

- **Ctrl+S:** Save all changes.

- **Ctrl+Z:** Undo the last operation.

- **Ctrl+Shift+Z:** Redo the last operation.

- **Ctrl+X / C / V:** Cut / Copy / Paste.

Real-life Example: While working on a project, you've made significant changes to your code. Using **Ctrl+S** becomes a quick reflex to ensure you save your progress without interrupting your flow.

Coding and Navigation

- **Ctrl+Space:** Basic code completion.

- **Ctrl+Shift+Space:** Smart code completion (filters the list of methods and variables by expected type).

- **Ctrl+B or Ctrl+Click:** Go to declaration (directly navigate to the code where a method or variable is declared).

- **Alt+Left/Right:** Navigate back / forward (useful when you've jumped to several locations and want to go back to where you were).

Real-life Example: Imagine you are exploring a large codebase with interconnected files. The Alt+Left/Right shortcut allows you to navigate back and forth between locations, making it easier to trace your steps.

Refactoring and Debugging

- **Shift+F6:** Rename a symbol.

- **Ctrl+Alt+M:** Extract a method (useful when you have a block of code you want to encapsulate in a new method).

- **F8:** Step over (in Debugger mode, execute the current line and go to the next one).

- **F7:** Step into (in Debugger mode, if the current line is a method call, go into the method and continue line-by-line debugging there).

Real-life Example: In the process of refactoring your code, you realize that a variable name no longer accurately reflects its purpose. The Shift+F6 shortcut allows you to rename the variable swiftly.

Version Control

- **Ctrl+K:** Commit changes.

- **Ctrl+T:** Update project from Version Control.

- **Ctrl+Alt+Z:** Undo the last Version Control action.

Real-life Example: You've implemented a new feature and want to commit your changes. Ctrl+K becomes your go-to shortcut to quickly initiate the commit process.

Remember, these are just a glimpse of the many shortcuts available in PyCharm. You can customize these shortcuts and even create your own in PyCharm's settings, tailoring the environment to your coding preferences and style.

Section 2: Introduce code completion and linting features.

Code Completion and Linting Features

Code Completion

Code completion is a powerful feature in PyCharm designed to enhance your coding speed and efficiency. As you begin typing, PyCharm automatically suggests and completes your code by proposing the remaining part of the variable, function, class, or keyword. This feature is context-aware, offering suggestions based on the current scope of your code.

 # When you start typing 'pri', PyCharm will suggest 'print'.

pri

Real-life Example: Imagine you're working on a program that involves complex mathematical calculations. Code completion in PyCharm accelerates the process by suggesting relevant functions and variables as you type, reducing the likelihood of syntax errors.

You can accept the suggestion by pressing Enter or Tab. This functionality not only expedites your coding process but also acts as a safeguard against typos and errors.

Linting Features

Linting, performed by a tool known as a linter, is the process of inspecting your source code for programmatic and stylistic errors. PyCharm incorporates several built-in linting features:

1. Syntax Highlighting: PyCharm uses different colors and fonts to highlight various parts of your code, making it visually appealing and easier to read and understand.

2. Error Detection: If there are errors in your code, PyCharm underlines them. Hovering over the error provides a description of the issue.

3. Quick Fixes: When PyCharm identifies an error, it often presents a lightbulb icon with quick fixes for the problem. Clicking on the lightbulb or pressing Alt+Enter reveals suggestions for resolving the issue.

 # PyCharm will underline 'prin' and suggest changing it to 'print.'

prin("Hello, World!")

Real-life Example: Consider you're working on a project with multiple collaborators, and one team member mistakenly uses an incorrect function name. PyCharm's quick fix suggestions allow for seamless collaboration by offering corrective measures without disrupting the workflow.

4. Code Inspections: PyCharm routinely inspects your code for potential problems. You can view all identified issues in the current file or project using the Problems tool window.

These features collectively assist you in writing cleaner, more consistent, and error-free code, fostering good coding practices and improving the overall quality of your projects.

Remember, these features in PyCharm are valuable companions on your coding journey, providing real-time assistance to ensure your code is both efficient and adheres to best practices.

Section 3: Explain version control basics, emphasizing the importance of saving work.

In this section, we will explore the basics of version control, a system that records changes to a file or set of files over time. This allows you to recall specific versions later, track changes, revert to previous stages, and collaborate on a project with others. It's like having a time machine for your code!

Why is Version Control Important?

Imagine you're working on a game and you've made a series of changes to your code. Suddenly, you realize that you've introduced a bug and you need to undo your changes. But you didn't save a backup copy! This is where version control comes in. It allows you to revert files back to a previous state, revert the entire project back to a previous state, compare changes over time, and more. It's like having an unlimited number of 'undo' steps!

For example, let's say you're working on a game and you decide to add a new feature. You spend hours coding it, but then you realize it's not working out. With version control, you can easily revert your code back to the state it was in before you started adding the feature.

How Does Version Control Work in PyCharm?

PyCharm has built-in support for version control systems like Git. Here's a basic workflow:

Initialize a Repository

A repository is like a database that stores your files and their revision history. You can create a new repository in PyCharm through `VCS -> Import into Version Control -> Create Git Repository`.

Make Changes

Write some code! As you make changes to your files, PyCharm will track these changes. It's like having a personal assistant who **Remember**s everything you do!

Commit Changes

Once you're satisfied with your changes, you can commit them. Committing is like taking a snapshot of your project at a point in time. You can do this in PyCharm through `VCS -> Git -> Commit File...`.

Push Changes

If you're working on a shared project, you can push your changes to the remote repository. This allows others to see and use your changes. You can do this in PyCharm through `VCS -> Git -> Push`.

Remember, version control is not just for coding! It's a good habit to get into for any documents that change over time. For example, if you're writing a story or a report for school, you can use version control to save different versions of your work and go back to them if needed.

CHAPTER 9: BUILDING YOUR FIRST PROJECT

Section 1: Plan Your Project and Set the Stage for Coding Adventures

Before diving into the coding adventure, it's crucial to plan your project. This involves understanding the problem you're trying to solve, breaking it down into smaller tasks, and deciding on the tools and technologies you'll use.

Understand the Problem:

The first step in planning your project is to understand the problem you're trying to solve. What is the goal of your project? What features do you want to include? Who is your target audience? For example, if you're creating a game, you need to know what kind of game it is, what the rules are, and who will be playing it. Answering these questions will help you define the scope of your project and guide your decision-making process.

Break Down the Problem:

Once you understand the problem, the next step is to break it down into smaller, manageable tasks. This process, known as decomposition, makes the problem easier to tackle. Each task should be a self-contained piece of work that contributes to the overall goal of the project. For instance, if you're creating a game, some tasks might include designing characters, creating game levels, and programming game mechanics.

Choose Your Tools:

Next, decide on the tools and technologies you'll use. For this book, we'll be using Python as our programming language and PyCharm as our Integrated Development Environment (IDE).

Python is a great language for beginners due to its readability and simplicity, and PyCharm provides many helpful features like code completion, error detection, and debugging tools. These tools will be your trusty companions on your coding adventure!

Set Up Your Environment:

Before you start coding, you'll need to set up your development environment. This involves installing Python and PyCharm, and setting up a new project in PyCharm. Make sure to organize your files and folders in a way that makes sense to you. A well-organized project is easier to understand and maintain. Think of it like organizing your room - it's much easier to find what you need when everything is in its place!

Start Coding:

Now that you've planned your project, it's time to start coding! **Remember**, coding is an iterative process. Don't worry if you don't get everything right the first time. Make a plan, write some code, test it out, and then improve it. Don't be afraid to make mistakes - that's how you learn! It's like building a LEGO set - sometimes you need to rearrange the pieces until everything fits together just right.

Remember, the journey of a thousand miles begins with a single step. So, let's take that first step together and embark on our coding adventure!

Section 2: Guide Children Through Writing and Testing Code, Debugging, and Improving Their Creations.

In this section, we'll guide you through the process of writing, testing, debugging, and improving your code. Think of it as a journey where each step brings you closer to your destination - a working program!

Writing Code:

The first step in creating a program is to write the code. In Python, we write instructions for the computer to follow. Here's an example of a simple Python program:

```python
print("Hello, World!")
```

This program prints the text "Hello, World!" to the console. It's like teaching your computer to greet the world!

Testing Code:

After writing code, it's important to test it to make sure it works as expected. This involves running the program and checking the output. In PyCharm, you can run your program by clicking on the green arrow in the top right corner. It's like giving your program a rehearsal before the big show!

Debugging Code:

If your program doesn't work as expected, you'll need to debug it. Debugging involves finding and fixing errors in your code. PyCharm provides many tools to help with debugging, such as breakpoints and step-by-step execution.

Here's how you can debug a program in PyCharm:

1. Set a breakpoint at a line of code by clicking next to the line number.

2. Run your program in debug mode by clicking on the bug icon in the top right corner.

3. Step through your code line by line, watching how the values of variables change and where the program goes wrong.

It's like being a detective, searching for clues to solve the mystery of why your program isn't working!

Improving Code:

Once your program works correctly, you might want to improve it. This could involve making it run more efficiently, adding new features, or making the code easier to read. Here are some ways to improve your code:

- **Use descriptive variable names:** This makes your code easier to understand. It's like naming your pets - the names help you identify them!

- **Add comments:** Comments can explain what your code does and why you wrote it that way. It's like leaving notes for your future self and others who read your code!

- **Remove unnecessary code:** If some parts of your code aren't needed, it's better to remove them. It's like cleaning up your room - it's easier to navigate when there's no clutter!

- **Use functions to avoid repeating code:** If you find yourself writing the same code multiple times, it's often a good idea to put that code into a function. It's like using a magic spell to do a task instantly!

Remember, coding is a process of continuous learning and improvement. Don't be discouraged if your code isn't perfect the first time. Keep practicing, keep experimenting, and most importantly, have fun! It's like building a sandcastle - sometimes it takes a few tries to get it just right, but the process is part of the fun!

CHAPTER 10: BEYOND THE BASICS - EXPLORING THE WORLD

Section 1: Showcase Real-World Projects: Games, Animations, Data Analysis, Web Scraping

Real-World Projects with Python and PyCharm

Games:

Python is a versatile language that can be used to create a variety of games, from simple number guessing games to complex graphical games. Here's an example of a number guessing game:

```
import random

number_to_guess = random.randint(1, 10)

print("Welcome to the number guessing game!")
print("I'm thinking of a number between 1 and 10.")

while True:
    player_guess = int(input("Your guess: "))
    if player_guess == number_to_guess:
        print("Good job! You guessed it!")
        break
    else:
        print("Sorry, try again.")
```

This game is a fun way to introduce the concept of loops and conditionals. In real life, this logic is used in many applications, such as automated testing or AI-based decision-making.

Animations:

Python can also be used to create animations. Libraries like turtle provide a simple way to create graphics. Here's an example:

```
import turtle

win = turtle.Screen()
win.bgcolor("black")

star = turtle.Turtle()
star.color("red")

star.speed(10)

for i in range(50):
    star.forward(100)
    star.right(144)

turtle.done()
```

This script creates a star animation. In real life, Python is used in animation industries for creating graphics and visual effects.

Data Analysis:

Python is widely used in data analysis. Libraries like pandas and matplotlib make it easy to manipulate data and create visualizations. Here's an example:

```python
import pandas as pd
import matplotlib.pyplot as plt

# Load data
data = pd.read_csv('data.csv')

# Analyze data
average = data['column1'].mean()

# Visualize data
data['column1'].plot(kind='hist')
plt.show()
```

This script loads a dataset, calculates the average of a column, and visualizes the data. In real life, Python is used in fields like finance, marketing, and science to analyze and visualize data.

Web Scraping:

Python can be used to scrape data from websites. Libraries like BeautifulSoup and requests make this task easier. Here's an example:

```python
from bs4 import BeautifulSoup
import requests

# Make a request to the website
response = requests.get("http://www.example.com")
soup = BeautifulSoup(response.text, 'html.parser')
```

```
# Find a specific element using its tag name and (optionally) its
attributes
element = soup.find("div", attrs={"class": "class-name"})

print(element.text)
```

This script retrieves data from a website and extracts specific information. In real life, web scraping is used in many fields, such as data mining, data processing, and testing.

Remember, these are just examples. The possibilities with Python and PyCharm are endless, limited only by your imagination and creativity.

Section 2: Provide Starting Points and Resources for Further Exploration Based on Interests.

Starting Points and Resources for Further Exploration

Once you've grasped the basics of Python and PyCharm, an exciting journey awaits with numerous directions to explore and expand your knowledge and skills. Here are some starting points and resources tailored to different areas of interest:

Game Development:

If you're fascinated by game development, dive into libraries like Pygame, a set of Python modules specifically crafted for creating video games.

Resource:

[Pygame Documentation](https://www.pygame.org/documentation)

Real-life Example: Imagine creating your own interactive game where a character navigates through a maze, collecting points while avoiding obstacles. Pygame empowers you to bring such imaginative ideas to life.

Web Development:

For those intrigued by web development, explore frameworks like Django and Flask. Django, a high-level Python web framework, promotes rapid development and embraces clean, pragmatic design principles, making it an excellent choice for building robust web applications.

Resource: [Django Documentation](https://docs.djangoproject.com/)

Real-life Example: Picture designing a personal website showcasing your coding projects and achievements. Django simplifies web development, allowing you to focus on creating a visually appealing and functional site.

Data Science:

If data science captivates you, delve into libraries like pandas for data manipulation and analysis, and matplotlib for data visualization.

Resources:

- **[Pandas Documentation]**(https://pandas.pydata.org/pandas-docs/stable/)

- **[Matplotlib Documentation]**(https://matplotlib.org/stable/contents.html)

Real-life Example: Consider analyzing a dataset containing information about weather patterns. Pandas helps you clean and structure the data, while Matplotlib allows you to visualize trends and patterns.

Machine Learning:

For those intrigued by machine learning, explore scikit-learn for various algorithms and tools. Delve into deeper realms with TensorFlow and PyTorch for deep learning applications.

Resources:

- [Scikit-learn Documentation](https://scikit-learn.org/stable/documentation.html)

- [TensorFlow Documentation](https://www.tensorflow.org/guide)

- [PyTorch Documentation](https://pytorch.org/docs/stable/index.html)

Real-life Example: Imagine creating a machine learning model that predicts housing prices based on different features. Scikit-learn provides a variety of algorithms to experiment with, enhancing your understanding of predictive modeling.

Competitive Programming:

If the thrill of problem-solving ignites your interest, platforms like Codeforces, AtCoder, and LeetCode offer a stage for participating in contests and honing your problem-solving skills.

Resources:

- [Codeforces](https://codeforces.com/)

- [AtCoder](https://atcoder.jp/)

- [LeetCode](https://leetcode.com/)

Real-life Example: Engage in a Codeforces contest where you're challenged to solve algorithmic problems within a time limit. This not only sharpens your coding skills but also introduces you to diverse problem-solving techniques.

Remember, the essence of learning programming is through hands-on experience. Select a project aligned with your interests, and let the coding adventure unfold!

CHAPTER 11: CONCLUSION

Section 1: Summary of Key Learnings

Key Learnings

Throughout this book, we've embarked on an exciting journey into the world of Python programming and explored the features of PyCharm. Here are some key learnings:

1. Python Fundamentals: We've learned about the basics of Python, including variables, data types, operators, control flow, and functions. These are the building blocks of any Python program.

Real-life Example: Think of variables as containers in which you can store different things. For instance, you might have a variable named `ice_cream_flavor`, and you can change its value to represent your current favorite flavor.

2. PyCharm Features: We've discovered how PyCharm can assist us in writing Python code, with features like code completion, debugging tools, refactoring code, and using version control.

Real-life Example: Imagine you're writing a program, and you want to use a specific function from a library. PyCharm's code completion suggests the function names as you type, saving you from memorizing every detail.

3. Data Structures: We've delved into Python's built-in data structures like lists, tuples, and dictionaries, understanding how they store data and how we can manipulate this data.

Real-life Example: Consider a scenario where you have a list of your favorite books. Python lists help you organize this information, and you can easily add or remove books as your preferences change.

4. File I/O and Error Handling: We've seen how Python interacts with files and how to handle errors in our code, which are crucial skills for building robust programs.

Real-life Example: Think of file I/O like managing a diary. You can write information to it (writing to a file) and read from it (reading from a file). Error handling is like having a backup plan in case you forget to write something or make a mistake.

5. Real-World Projects: We've looked at how Python can be used to create games, animations, perform data analysis, and even scrape data from websites.

Real-life Example: Imagine creating a simple game where you control a character jumping over obstacles. This involves using Python to handle player input, update the game state, and display graphics.

6. Planning and Improving Code: We've learned the importance of planning our projects, testing and debugging our code, and continuously seeking to improve our creations.

Real-life Example: Think of coding like crafting a story. Planning ensures you have a plot, testing helps you catch plot holes, and continuous improvement is like refining your story based on feedback.

7. Further Exploration: We've provided starting points for further exploration in areas like game development, web development, data science, machine learning, and competitive programming.

Real-life Example: Suppose you enjoy solving puzzles. Competitive programming platforms offer a space where you can challenge yourself with algorithmic problems, honing your problem-solving skills.

Remember, the journey of learning to code is a marathon, not a sprint. It's about continuous learning and improvement. Don't be afraid to make mistakes - that's how you learn. Keep practicing, keep experimenting, and most importantly, have fun!

Section 2: The Next Steps in Your Python Journey

The Next Steps in Your Python Journey

Congratulations on completing this book and embarking on your Python coding adventure! You've learned the basics of Python, explored the features of PyCharm, and even created some real-world projects. But the journey doesn't end here. Here are some next steps you can take to continue your Python journey:

1. Deepen Your Python Knowledge:

While you've learned the basics of Python, there's still much more to explore. You can delve deeper into topics like object-oriented programming, advanced data structures, decorators, generators, and more. There are many online resources and books available to help you deepen your Python knowledge.

Real-life Example: If you've enjoyed creating games, diving into object-oriented programming can empower you to design more complex and interactive game systems.

2. Explore Python Libraries:

Python has a rich ecosystem of libraries that can help you do everything from web development to data analysis to machine learning and more. Some libraries to explore include Django for web development, NumPy and pandas for data analysis, and TensorFlow and scikit-learn for machine learning.

Real-life Example: Consider a scenario where you want to build a website showcasing your projects. Django simplifies web development, allowing you to focus on the content and functionality.

3. Work on Projects:

The best way to learn programming is by doing. Come up with a project that interests you and start building. It could be a game, a website, a data analysis project, or anything else you're passionate about. Working on projects will help you apply what you've learned and gain practical coding experience.

Real-life Example: Suppose you're interested in space. You could work on a project that retrieves and visualizes data about planets, moons, and asteroids.

4. Join the Python Community:

The Python community is a great place to learn, share, and collaborate with other Python enthusiasts. You can join Python meetups, participate in coding challenges, contribute to open-source projects, and more. Being part of a community can make your coding journey more enjoyable and rewarding.

Real-life Example: Imagine participating in a coding challenge where you collaborate with others to solve a problem. It's not just about the solution; it's about the shared experience of learning and growing together.

Remember, learning to code is a journey, not a destination. Embrace the challenges, celebrate your successes, and enjoy the continuous adventure of discovering the endless possibilities that Python coding offers!

EPILOGUE

And so, our adventure comes to an end. But remember, every end is just a new beginning. You've journeyed through the world of "Coding Adventures with Python and PyCharm for Kids: Unlocking the Magic of Coding: A Kid's Guide to Python Adventures with PyCharm", and along the way, you've unlocked the magic of coding.

You've learned to speak Python, to wield PyCharm, and to create with code. You've faced challenges, solved problems, and brought your ideas to life. You've become a coder.

But this is just the start. The world of coding is vast and ever-changing. There are always new languages to learn, new problems to solve, and new adventures to embark on.

So, keep coding. Keep learning. Keep creating. And most importantly, keep having fun. Because that's what coding is all about.

Until our next adventure, happy coding!

ABOUT THE AUTHOR

Ghada Atef

Ghada Atef is a seasoned Linux and Python expert with a passion for open-source technologies. With a deep understanding of various Linux distributions and their applications, she has authored several comprehensive guides and practice exams to help aspiring Linux professionals.

Her works include:

1. "Unofficial Red Hat RHCSA 9 (EX200) Exam Preparation 2023: Six Complete RHCSA 9 (EX200) Practice Exams with Answers (Third Edition)" - The third edition of the comprehensive guide to the RHCSA 9 (EX200) exam, featuring six complete practice exams.
2. "Mastering Ansible: A Comprehensive Guide to Automating Configuration Management and Deployment" - A detailed exploration of Ansible, providing practical knowledge on automating configuration management and deployment.
3. "Mastering Ubuntu: A Comprehensive Guide to Linux's Favorite" - An in-depth guide to using and mastering Ubuntu, one of the most popular Linux distributions.
4. "Unofficial Red Hat Certified System Administrator RHCSA 8 & 9 (EX200) Exam Preparation 2023: Six Complete RHCSA 8 & 9 Practice Exams with Answers" - A thorough preparation guide for the RHCSA 8 & 9 (EX200) exam, featuring six complete practice

exams.

5. "RHCE EX294 Mastery: Six Practice Exams for Exam Success" - A comprehensive guide offering detailed answers to ace the Red Hat Certified Engineer EX294 Exam.

6. "Unofficial Red Hat RHCSA 9 (EX200) Exam Preparation 2023: Master the Red Hat RHCSA 9 (EX200) Exam with Confidence" - An online course designed to build confidence and knowledge for the RHCSA 9 (EX200) exam.

Ghada's work is characterized by its practical approach, clear explanations, and real-world relevance. Her dedication to helping others master Linux is evident in the depth and breadth of her work. Whether you're a beginner just starting out or a seasoned professional looking to validate your skills, Ghada's books and courses are an invaluable resource on your journey.

THANK YOU!